Fostering Innovations in Students

Fostering Innovations in Students

Vigyan Ratna Lakshman Prasad

Published by
PRABHAT PRAKASHAN PVT. LTD.
4/19 Asaf Ali Road,
New Delhi-110 002 (INDIA)
e-mail: prabhatbooks@gmail.com

ISBN 978-93-5186-800-2
FOSTERING INNOVATIONS IN STUDENTS
by Shri Vigyan Ratna Lakshman Prasad

Edition
2025

Price
₹ 250.00 (Rupees Two Hundred Fifty only)

Printed at
Shree Sai Printers, Sahibabad

This book is dedicated with great respect to

Hon'ble Late Dr. A.P.J. Abdul Kalam

Former President of India

Why Innovations are Needed

(Start a New Era of Innovations and Innovators)

The developing societies worldwide have a heavy agenda. They must banish poverty which stalks them. Some three billion people are below the poverty line and 70% of the world's poor live in rural areas. In India, 750 million people are living in villages.

The tasks of removing unemployment, illiteracy and diseases are equally formidable and challenging. The quality of life of half of the world's population is an anachronism in the Twenty-first Century.

Low productivity and poverty are synonymous. High productivity comes from value creation; and value creation from innovation. In the past, resource deficiency was a major constraint. In the new knowledge society, resource is substituted by knowledge. The amalgam of innovation and information are the two major inputs of the futuristic knowledge society.

Innovation is the only effective response to the problems of the developing societies. Innovation alone can accelerate their growth, enabling them to catch up with the western world.

In the era of globalization, the only way India can face the onslaught of competition is by becoming creative, innovative and compassionate towards the disadvantaged communities and individuals living in rural area. There is a need to start a new era of innovations and innovators in our country. It is the need of the hour to tap the potential talents existing in rural India as well as in the urban society.

Wake Up Indian Youth

(*To Transform India Through Innovations*)

Every drop fills an ocean.
Every wave makes a sea.
That's how valuable innovations are,
To this World!
There is an ocean full of innovations,
Waiting to be done at any point of time.
Innovations small or big are equally important.
Even grassroots innovations are no less important.
Every creative idea we conceive,
Every innovation we make,
Will help make life a bit easier.
From little to much.
The future is full of challenges.
Let us take them in stride.
Let us bow to make a difference.
Not just flow with the tide.
With perseverance alone,
The results we will see.
Every innovation big or small, counts.
Can that transform the India?
YES!!!
So wake up and do.

—Lakshman Prasad

Foreword

Innovation **and** *innovators* are buzz words that have been attracting all segments of global society since the dawn of time. Contrary to popular belief, innovation is not restricted to industrialists, technologists and artists; rather, common people who have an innovative streak develop into major contributors to specific fields. Awareness about recent developments, acquisition of related knowledge and skills, and incorporating the latest practices into industry have become the essential ingredient for the success of every individual, organization and nation at large. More than ever before, in this Intellectual Property Right Age, we live in a society that values and respects innovation.

That every individual can participate in the mission of innovation is the message of this book written by a distinguished innovator Vigyan Ratna Lakshman Prasad. Creativity cannot be confined to the boundaries of gender, age, place and time. That is the essence of this book. In this book, the intricacy of innovation is dealt within a simple manner. The book covers all the aspects starting from definitions, processes and nomenclature of innovations to the issues of feasibility, relevance and economics of innovation. The author has pleaded for creating an environment in educational institutions from the primary level to the highest level so as to draw out the creativity of students at an early age and making innovative thinking a standard modus operandi as opposed to an occasional, situational, goal-driven exercise.

The rich experience of the author in the area of research and development activities has helped him to cover all the practical attributes of the innovations, patents and commercialization of ideas. The significance of nomenclature of innovations and the maintenance of an innovator diary are important topics that are presented objectively. With extremely relevant examples, the author demonstrates how ignoring these aspects of innovation may cost the innovators heavily. Innovations do not always require heavy investments – this is all the more reason for every student and small-scale business-owner to read this book and make every little idea of theirs count for its maximum possible value. Of particular relevance to them is the chapter on resources and incentives that are available to innovators, monetary or otherwise.

Reading at length about the innovations of many legendary achievers and tracing their journeys of excellence towards becoming business tycoons, scientists and entrepreneurs will be a great source of inspiration for readers. With his extraordinary background as a social worker, entrepreneur, scientist and technologist, Shri Lakshman Prasad does full justice to the selected topic. I am confident that the book will be able to break the mental barriers of the common man who believes that innovation is only for the extraordinarily gifted. It will inspire the reader of the book to look at innovation as merely a way of life, and get him to adopt it in his sphere of activity.

I congratulate Shri Lakshman Prasad for taking up a topic of utmost importance and presenting the dynamics of innovations in this manner.

—Prof. Satish Chandra Jain
Vice-Chancellor,
Mangalayatan University,
Aligarh.

Author's Note

Realizing the role and importance of innovations in meeting stiff global competition and removing poverty, illiteracy and decease thereby improving life of rural population, Hon'ble Prime Minister of India, Dr. Manmohan Singh declared on 3rd January, 2010, while inaugurating the 97th Session of Indian Science Congress, that the present Decade-2010-2020 would be the **"Decade of Innovation".** Earlier on 4th June 2009, Her Excellency Smt. Pratibha Devi Singh Patil, President of India also declared in the Parliament that the Decade of 2010-2020 would be observed as "Decade of Innovation". It appears that both Hon'ble Prime Minister and the President of India have resolved to making India an innovative society thereby making India a developed nation by 2020. Impressed by the above declaration, I have tried to write this small book in an innovative manner in the form of questions and answers so that our students may easily understand the basics/fundamentals of innovation thereby getting some novel ideas to involve in innovation adventurism.

Innovative society cannot be made overnight nor innovative culture can be inculcated amongst the people in a short span of time. Launching an innovation movement is imperative to foster the spirit of innovation amongst all sections of society, particularly the students from primary stage to university level. A few years back Former President of India, Dr. A.P.J. Abdul Kalam in his message on "International Innovation Day", communicated that "Learning leads to acquisition of knowledge which blossom into original thinking. Thinking leads to creativity. Creativity results in innovations. The seed of innovations are laid when one begins to question – why, how and why not. Therefore, children must be encouraged to question so as to encourage their creativity and innovative spirits".

Greatly impressed by Dr. Kalam's ideas and views, fortunately I have interacted with more than one lakh students of various schools, colleges and universities ranging from High-School, Intermediate, Graduate, Post-graduate, MBA, and Engineering during last 15 years or so. Thus, I got the opportunity to talk to them freely and frankly on various aspects related with innovations. I noticed that many students were interested and enthusiastic to get involved in innovative exercise but they did need proper help and guidance. Therefore, requirement of such type of books cannot be ignored. Rather such type of literature will be much more needed in future preparing a large number of students innovators for obvious advantages.

The book briefly and clearly deals with subjects related with definition of science and technology; discovery, invention, innovation; creativity and innovation; education and innovation; area of innovations; process of innovations; nomenclature of innovations; innovator diary; benefits from innovations; recognition, awards and honours etc.

In the end, Author has only one submission to make: If this work evokes some interest in the young readers and turn even one student an innovator, then he would consider that his labour of writing this book is amply rewarded.

—Lakshman Prasad
3/6, Marris Road,
Mendu Compound,
Aligarh-202001, U.P.

Acknowledgements

First of all I would like to start by thanking Almighty God for giving me mental faculties to write this small book about the not much written subject in our country.

I am very grateful and express my gratitude to Prof. S.C. Jain, Vice-Chancellor, Mangalayatan University, Aligarh for writing an inspiring Foreword to this book.. His encouraging words and blessings have added an enormous value to this book.

My sincere thanks are due to my friends, well-wishers, associates and colleagues for the encouragement they have given me throughout the preparation of this book. My thanks are also due to the learned readers of my earlier published books on innovation/invention for offering some useful and constructive suggestions for incorporating in my coming publications, some of their valuable and useful suggestions have been included in this book.

While writing this book, I have tried to utilize my mixed experiences of plight and pleasure encountered by me during conducting more than 20 innovations/ inventions during last 30 years. I have utilized some material for this book from my earlier published works viz., 'Making India Innovative', 'Sadharan Aavishkaron Kee Asadharan Saphaltayen', 'Aaiye Aavishkarak Baney', 'Bachchon Ke Priya Vastu ke

Avishkar'. 'Chatra-Chatragein: Kaise Innovator Baney aur Karorapati Bhee'. Similarly, I have also taken some material from Dr. A.P.J. Abdul Kalam's book "Indomitable Spirit". Therefore, it is my sacred duty to pay my special thanks to the publishers of these books.

I owe special duty to express my thanks to my journalist friend Mr. Sulakshan Mohan, living in Toronto, Canada and my another friend Mr. C.B. Agrawal for going through the manuscript and offering some valuable suggestions to improve the book.

My wife Uma, my both daughters Amita Agarwal and Vanita Kumar also deserve my sincere thanks for helping me to write this book. My granddaughter Anamika Bansal and grandsons Dhruv Kumar and Varun Kumar also deserve special thanks for helping me by providing some useful material for the book. I will fail in my duty if I do not pay my thanks to Mrs. Vijay Mittal for helping me to make the manuscripts worthy for publication.

—Lakshman Prasad

Contents

1
Child Mind

Child mind is like a ball of raw earth that may be shaped in such a way as one may like. The child has a strong tendency of learning, understanding as well as copying.
He learns mostly from his surroundings. His mother and then his father is his first school. He ventures to learn about eatables, toys, games and on further growing up a little about the house and modern equipments present in his vicinity.

In a case of natural growth of children, it is thus necessary that the things present around them must be brought to their notice. As per present requirements, it is of course necessary that children should be physically healthy. It is also necessary to develop a scientific and innovative attitude in them. This mental tendency would create a capacity to do novel things necessary for any country, particularly for developing nations. In this age of competition, it is necessary to prepare children for a novel act in such a manner as the players are prepared for Olympic Games from their childhood.

Children's favourites are eatables. In the modern age new eatable items like fast food etc. are readily available and children are very fond of them. If information on generation and growth of these food stuffs is brought to their knowledge they would adopt the same quickly. Similarly their second love is games and toys. The children often break and dismantle toys to satisfy the curiosity of knowing that what items create sound. They may be made familiar with the process of invention through these games-toys also.

Today a number of modern equipments are available in and out of the house. Several of them are used by children. Video games, computer, internet etc. are not beyond their reach. They often get opportunities to enjoy radio, T.V., animation films etc. It is also necessary to encourage children to use these articles and to narrate before them that how could those things be modified become useful.

Under modern system of teaching, there is a practice to teach them by means of games. Letters and numerical etc. are taught by means of games not only to ordinary children but success has been achieved in imparting working knowledge through it even to the mentally challenged children.

Thus, moving a step forward, scientific and innovative psychology may easily be developed. It has been a well-known fact that there is no minimum age for doing innovations. There are a number of people who became innovative in their childhood and performed wonders by novel methods/actions.

In the coming chapters, the questions related to innovation raised by students, both girls and boys, have been answered in a very simple way to satisfy their curiosity related to innovations, which would hopefully inspire them to do novel acts by novel methods in their career as well as it would improve their intellectual development and enhance their treasure of knowledge. Knowledge has always been regarded as power.

"Ignited young minds are a powerful resource. This resource is mighter than any resource on the earth, in the sky and under the sea."

—Dr. A.P.J. Abdul Kalam

"If you want to shine like a sun. First burn like a sun."

—Dr. A.P.J. Abdul Kalam

□

2
Innovation

Increasing usefulness of innovations at the end of 20th century and from the beginning of 21st century has been widely accepted by all the countries of the world. Mainly developing and developed nations are rapidly paying attention to the need of innovations in essential areas of their respective country. They are swiftly making efforts also to encourage the people particularly children and students as well as all sections of the society for providing more strength and speed to the innovative activities. It would prove to be helpful in finding solutions to their several economic needs and social problems.

In the course of detailed discussions with students on the subject recently, some students asked different types of questions in this regard.

Question: What is the difference between Science and Technology?

Answer: Science as moored in pure knowledge and directed towards basic understanding whereas technology is directed towards the usage.

Question: What is the function of the scientists and technologists?

Answer: It is not a role of the scientists to distinguish between what is commercially and materially useful and what is not, but the technologists are primarily interested in commercial viability of the idea.

Question: What is the significance of innovation?

Answer: Before knowing significance of innovation, we have to understand what is the difference between discovery, invention and innovation? People often do not easily distinguish these three and use one instead of the other inspite of the fact that the procedures of all the three are absolutely different.

Question: How is the innovation different from discovery and invention?

Answer: The procedures of discovery, invention and innovation are different in the following manner:

Discovery: A process already existing in the nature, but it is not known to general public and when it becomes known, it is called a discovery. For example the Archimedes theory of floating of objects, Newton's doctrine of gravity, Galileo making it known to all that Earth moves around the Sun, were discoveries, as these things were already going on in the nature.

Invention: Under this process, a new thing for the first time is produced. It was not made earlier. If two persons have made a new thing almost at the same time, the person who has made it first is recognized as an inventor. Second person remains deprived of both the credit as well as the patent.

In other words, to make a new thing or to develop a novel process is called invention. For example, making of electric bulb by Thomas Alva Edison, making of a telephone by Alexander Graham Bell, making of steam engine etc. before industrial revolution etc. are called inventions.

Innovation: Under this process, a new product or a new service or a new use is developed. When a thing, object, product, system, method is developed or modification in process is made, it is called innovation. In other words, when an object, a product and a novel method and technical change takes place in this process, when this technical change is accomplished for the first time this process is called innovation. In other words, when a product is improved and a novelty is brought to it and when it is made more useful for people for lesser costs, it is called innovation. In short, an improvement over any existing product/device/process is called innovation.

In today's context this act is considered very significant development for social change and economic growth across the world.

Question: What does innovation mean?

Answer: Innovation is a multidimensional and comprehensive concept. Where existing products, process and uses are so improved or novelties are brought so that their utility may enhance, cost may reduce, resources may be beneficially used, risks are lessened, standard of living is improved and ultimately the nation becomes prosperous.

Question: Does the word innovation is known by various names in Hindi language?

Answer: Yes. In fact the correct nomenclature of word "Innovation" prevalent in Hindi language is "*Navachar*" but the words such as *Navinikaran, Nav-Pravartan, Navonmesh* etc. are also in use. It may, therefore, be considered that it is known by various names in Hindi.

Questions

1. Railway Engine will be covered under which category? Innovation, invention or discovery?
2. Whether Electric Bulb will be called as an invention or innovation?
3. Whether finding of mars can be considered under the category of discovery?
4. Whether attachment of hand rest on both sides of chair can be called as an innovation?

"Knowledge without innovation is of no value. It is through the process of innovation along that knowledge is converted into wealth and social good. Innovators are those, who do not know that it cannot be done. Innovators are those who see that everyone else sees, but think of what no one else thinks. Innovators refuse status quo, they convert inspirations into solutions and ideas into products. Building such innovators will require an all – pervasive attitudinal change towards life and work—a shift from a culture of drift to a culture of dynamism, from a culture of idle prattle to a culture of thought and work, from diffidence, from despair to hope. Revival of Indian creativity and the innovative spirit needs to be made into a national movement today, in the same spirit and on the same scale as marked our freedom struggle. 'I' in India must stand for innovation."

—Dr. R.A. Mashelkar

Points to Ponder

1. Please write, first of all, the gist of this chapter and thereafter answer each and every question clearly.
2. In case of any clarification, please do consult your mentor or write to the author of this book at the address given at the end of this book.
3. Suggestion, if any, to improve this chapter may please be sent to the author.

□

3

Creativity and Innovation

Creativity has many dimensions such as inventions, discoveries and innovations. Creativity is the ability to imagine or invent something new by combining, changing or reapplying existing ideas. It is an attitude to accept change and newness, a willingness to play with ideas and possibilities, a flexibility of outlook, the habit of enjoying the good while looking for ways to improve it. Creativity is a process to work hard and continually improve ideas and solutions by making gradual alterations and refinements. The important aspect of creativity is; seeing the same thing as everybody else, but thinking of something different.

Question: Is the creativity found at a particular place/part of a country?

Answer: It may be found anywhere around the world. It may be found in a kitchen, playground, fisherman's hut, house of a farmer/labour, dairy farm, cattle breeding centre or it may emanate from classrooms, laboratories, industries, research, development centres etc.

Question: How can the creativity be promoted?

Answer: Seeds of creativity are inherent in the mind of every human being. However, the sincere efforts are required to be made to sprout the same. Each and every person is creative and each mind is inquisitive.

Question: How can curiosity of students/ children be satisfied?

Answer: Whenever a child/student asks a question we must answer it. It will satisfy his curiosity. It is the primary responsibility of every father/mother and teacher. If it is so done from childhood, creativity will be nourished and children will flourish. This will also promote a culture amongst children to answer the questions, when others ask them.

Question: Can the creativity bring some change in life patterns?

Answer: Many people found a change in their life with the support of creativity. Many people have developed many equipments/products which have altered the character of the world. There has been a revolution in the field of science and technology by means of several types of inventions/innovations made by scientist like Thomas Alva Edison. With the innovative idea of Mahatma Gandhi, the movement of non-violence sparked the war against British government and helped several countries in achieving their independence.

Question: Whether creativity can make an impossible a possibility?

Answer: What we have seen in science and technology in the last 60 years has proved that what was thought impossible once has happened and what is thought possibly has not yet happened but it certainly will happen. Particularly in the field of aeronautics, space technology, electronics, materials, computer science and software products, the world has progressed to new dimensions. The National Innovative Capacity is a country's critical potential to reinforce both its political and economic entity with commercially relevant competitive products in the global market place.

Question: Does creativity lead to innovation and wealth resulting into prosperity?

Answer: It is through the process of innovation that knowledge is converted into wealth. Innovation is a systematic, organized, rational work usually done in many stages like analysis, tests and experiments. Innovation needs courage to think different, courage to invent, courage to discover the impossible and courage to combat the problems and succeed.

Question: Is creativity the foundation of Human thinking?

Answer: Creativity is the foundation of human thinking and will always be at the highest end of the value chain irrespective of the growth of computers with respect to speed and memory. Creativity will continue to be the forte of humankind and enormous computing power, provided by technology. It would be an effective tool that the human mind will use to craft its plans to create a better world to live in.

Questions

1. Is creativity a heritage of a particular country?
2. How can the seeds of creativity be sprouted in students?
3. How can parents and teachers nurture creativity in students?
4. Is the creativity the foundation of human thinking? If so, how is useful for the society at large?

> *"There is a spark of inventiveness in all the human beings which, all too often, gets extinguished as they get caught up in the competitiveness of the examination system, and the pressures of daily life and work."*
>
> **—Sonia Gandhi**

> *"Creativity is just connecting things. When you ask creative people how they did something, they feel a little guilty because they did not really do it, they just saw something. It seemed obvious to them after a while. That is because they were able to connect experiences they have had and synthesize new things."*
>
> **—Steve Jobs**

Points to Ponder

1. Please write, first of all, the gist of this chapter and thereafter answer each and every question clearly.
2. In case of any clarification, please do consult your mentor or write to the author of this book at the address given at the end of this book.
3. Suggestion, if any, to improve this chapter may please be sent to the author.

□

4

Who can Innovate?

Many people say that the society has been benefited greatly by inventions. But rarely there are very few persons who think about the innovations. How innovations have come into existence and how do they happen and who can do them. How they have benefitted the community at large.
In this connection, an intelligent girl asked the following questions in order to remove her doubts.

Question: Who is called an innovator and how is he different from others?

Answer: An innovator is a person who sees what others see but he thinks which others do not think. In other words, his thinking on problems is different from that of others. He is relatively more sensitive towards the problems and endeavours to resolve them. Sensitivity is the mother of creativity.

Question: Is there any age limit prescribed for doing innovation?

Answer: There is no age limit for doing innovation and any person can innovate at any age. A person of any age and class can be an innovator. The creativity or new thinking is not limited to any age or class. It may come in the childhood and may continue till old age.

Question: Whether only man can do innovations?

Answer: This assumption is totally baseless. Any man or woman, boy or girl can do innovations.

Question: Whether a boy and a student can take part in the field of innovation?

Answer: Any student, a boy as well as a girl, can actively participate in this sphere as young children have open minds. They have no prejudices and have no apprehensions that this could not be done or it would have no benefits. They can and do novel things, while playing games which may prove to be useful.

Question: Whether a physically challenged person can be an innovator?

Answer: The physically challenged has no obstruction in working in the field of innovation. Even he may become a good innovator. Many specially a bled persons have done several useful innovations and served the society.

Question: Whether teachers in schools and colleges can contribute to the field of innovations?

Answer: The school and college teachers have ample opportunities. They can participate comprehensively in the field of innovation. Moreover, devoted teachers can, with hard work and dedication can sow the seeds of innovative culture amongst the students successfully.

Question: Whether even a professional can take part in the field of innovation?

Answer: Since professionals are preoccupied, they are unable to devote much attention and time in this field. But it should not be taken that they cannot become innovators. In foreign countries as well as in our own country, some advocates and judges, doctors and surgeons, chartered accountants and auditors, managers and technocrats etc. have also contributed a lot to the field of innovation and they have promoted the innovations by modifying several types of systems, methods, proceedings etc. Some engineers and technologists are also making significant contribution in the field of innovation by developing and manufacturing new equipments, gadgets etc.

Question: In the sphere of innovation, I have so far poor knowledge. Can I ever succeed in doing innovation?

Answer: In case your knowledge in the field of innovation is nil and you are ignorant about it, it does not matter. In future you can do innovation. Be a keen observant about things and events happening around you and think to improve upon them and then make efforts, you can become an innovator. We can do innovations by making radical changes in our living styles, dresses, eatables, conducts and morals. You can innovate in order to improve standard of the living of poor, orphans, and be a keen observant. You can do innovation by creating good equipments for physically and mentally challenged people to make their lives easy. There are several areas where you can contribute to the field of innovation with your diligence.

Nobody should ever feel small or helpless. As Former President of India Dr. A.P.J. Abdul Kalam said, "We all are born with a divine fire in us. Our efforts should be to give wings to this fire and fill the world with glow of its goodness".

Questions

1. How is an innovator different from other people?
2. Is creativity or novel thinking bound to the limit of age?
3. Whether a sensitive person can only succeed in doing innovations?
4. What virtues are required to be a successful innovator?
5. What is the message given by Dr. A.P.J. Abdul Kalam?

> *"Men and Women who have ideas and objectives before them and the urge to achieve them, do not wait for the turn of fortune's wheel."*
>
> **—Jawaharlal Nehru**

> *"Failure will never overtake me if my determination to succeed is strong enough."*
>
> **—Dr. A.P.J. Abdul Kalam**

> *"Innovator do not exist just in formal laboratories. Millions of them exist in villages, in homes and on the streets. To encourage community innovation, it is necessary to scout, support, spawn and scale up the grass roots innovation."*
>
> **—Dr. R.A. Mashelkar**

Points to Ponder

1. Please write, first of all, the gist of this chapter and thereafter answer each and every question clearly.
2. In case of any clarification, please do consult your mentor or write to the author of this book at the address given at the end of this book.
3. Suggestion, if any, to improve this chapter may please be sent to the author.

□

5

The Education and Innovation

There is a general assumption that an educated person alone can innovate and illiterate man and woman cannot succeed in doing innovations. This assumption is absolutely wrong. Although, education helps in furthering thought process and making it sharp, yet even lesser educated persons with determination can successfully innovate for which qualities like absolute sensitivity, sincerity, honesty and diligence are needed. Therefore, there is a necessity to remove this misconception.

The education has its vital role for working in any field. Learning leads to acquisition of knowledge which blossoms into original thinking. Thinking leads to creativity. Creativity results in innovations. The seeds of innovation are laid when one begins to question why, how, and why not. Therefore, children must be encouraged to question so as to encourage their creativity and innovative spirits.

In this regard some students asked the questions as follows:

Question: Whether special technical education is required for doing innovation?

Answer: The innovation is a process for which special technical education is not essential. Of course, the technical education does help in enhancing nurturing our thought process and contemplation and helps in accelerating the process of innovation.

Question: Whether ordinary education is needed for an innovation?

Answer: Education proves to be helpful in nurturing thought process. But ordinary education is not absolutely necessary for doing an innovation.

Illiterate farmers and artisans of several countries of the world have made several types of small innovations, which not only made their respective occupation easy but helped them to working more speedily and efficiently. Thus, the labour cost came down.

Question: Is the innovation subject being promoted in the foreign countries?

Answer: Development of innovation almost in all western countries is being encouraged in keeping in view the increasing significance and usefulness of innovations. Few years ago, Russia first of all introduced the innovation as a subject in the school syllabus.

Similarly, certain universities in England have introduced Post-Graduate Degree Course in 'Innovation' some years ago.

Question: Would it be proper and useful to introduce the subject of innovation in Indian schools?

Answer: Keeping in view the modern needs of India, there is not only need to accelerate pace of innovations but to think seriously to introduce the subject of innovation in our schools. Therefore to promote innovative activities, students should be selected at the school level and should be encouraged to participate in innovative activities. It would help making India a developed nation.

Question: What type of programms should be organized in schools so that students can be attracted towards the innovation?

Answer: At present, in all the developing countries of the world, emphasis is being laid on enhancing scientific awareness. Therefore, if we make efforts to develop scientific and inventive temper in our students from the very childhood, our children could successfully become good scientists, inventors and innovators in their careers. Even the students from our rural areas are not lacking in talents. What is required is that these unknown talents should be brought before the society which will help in boosting morale of the rural talents. Therefore, an "Innovation Club" or "Innovation Samiti", should be established in each and every school so that the students may transform their creative and constructive ideas into products. The students should be honoured and rewarded for their novel activities.

Questions

1. Whether an illiterate and undereducated people can do innovations? If so, what type of

virtues and characteristics should be inherent in them?

2. Whether a person can succeed in innovating without an original thinking?
3. How can the children be infused with innovative spirits from their childhood?
4. How can the unknown talents be identified and encouraged?
5. Whether the innovation area would be strengthened by including the 'innovation' subject in the school syllabus?

> *"All of us do not have equal talent. But, all of us have an equal opportunity to develop our talents."*
>
> **—Dr. A.P.J. Abdul Kalam**

> *"People can be motivated to creativity, simply with the instruction to be creative."*
>
> **—Richard Saul Wurman**

Points to Ponder

1. Please write, first of all, the gist of this chapter and thereafter answer each and every question clearly.
2. In case of any clarification, please do consult your mentor or write to the author of this book at the address given at the end of this book.
3. Suggestion, if any, to improve this chapter may please be sent to the author.

□

6
The Area of Innovation

Some people think that all the necessary inventions and innovations have already been made in all the areas. Therefore, no such area is left where there is a scope for further innovations. This idea is not only wrong but also unwise and such thinking is negative. Similarly, some people say that innovation can be done in technical areas only. Such an assumption is also wrong. The area of innovation is not only wide but also unlimited as innovations can be made in all the activities relating to the life.
In this regard, few children asked following questions in order to satisfy their inquisitiveness.

Question: What are the areas in which innovations can be made?

Answer: As stated earlier, the area of innovation is very vast and unlimited. Innovations may be made in various fields such as science and technology, power and electricity, water, traffic, telecommunication, education, agriculture, medical, space, road and buildings, economic and social, cultural, political, law, sports, entertainment, administration, crime and law, religious and spiritual etc.

India being a pro-agriculture country, there are numerous opportunities for innovations in the agriculture and agriculture-related areas, which call for deep consideration and operation.

Question: Can you name the areas where innovative products and things etc. can be successfully commercialized and merchandized?

Answer: Mainly foodstuffs, child toys, brainy indoor games, adventurous games to be played on plains and hills, modern machines of different types and medical health equipments, transport-related means, kitchen appliances, clothing, office material, farming and gardening equipments, personal security and national security-related appliances etc.

Besides, there are several unexplored and unknown areas where innovations are called for. The process of innovation would incessantly continue till mankind exists on this earth. Therefore, there is need to think of such areas in which innovations have not so far been attempted.

Questions

1. Is the area of innovation very vast? If so, state certain fields where innovations are badly required?

2. What types of innovations are required in the field of agriculture so as to make the farming operation easy and simple?
3. Whether women can only innovate in the areas of foodstuffs?

> *"All Birds find shelter during a rain. But Eagle avoids rain by flying above the Clouds."*
>
> **—Dr. A.P.J. Abdul Kalam**

> *"There is an ocean full of innovations waiting to be done at any point of the time."*
>
> **—Prof. Yash Pal**

Points to Ponder

1. Please write, first of all, the gist of this chapter and thereafter answer each and every question clearly.
2. In case of any clarification, please do consult your mentor or write to the author of this book at the address given at the end of this book.
3. Suggestion, if any, to improve this chapter may please be sent to the author.

□

7
Process of Innovation

> The innovation is something new which has not happened earlier. In other words, we may understand that creativity leads to innovation. In the case of an innovation, an act, a thing is done differently. The creativity also means to create such new things, works or ideas as were unknown earlier.

Question: How many types of innovations exist and how the same are classified?

Answer: In view of the generality of innovation process, it is divided into three major categories for the purpose of its study:

1. **Simple Innovations:** These are called petty improvements or nut-bolt improvement. These innovations may be performed by any ordinary person, woman, child, student, artisan etc. It requires no special education/training.

   In children, innovative or creativity is inherent by birth because of their curiosity and inquisitiveness. There is a need to discover their hidden talents and to boost their innovative talents.

2. **Comprehensive Innovations:** Are those where comprehensive changes are carried out by concentrated efforts. This change is so effective that it alters the character of the industry. Through such innovations, a product is refined, cost is reduced, quality is improved and production line is expanded. The motors/cars/buses/trucks/aircrafts etc. have changed the form of transportation and movement from one place to an other place has become very fast, easy and comfortable.
3. **Advanced Technological Innovations:** Are those which bring improvement in complex machinery in a planned manner. Such technological innovations include the complex machinery, communication network, ordinance equipments and space exploration. Technical changes are constantly taking place. This type of phase runs for a long period of time and the work continuous for years. The people working in a number of different disciplines participate there. It also incurs heavy costs. These are long-term and very important and critical schemes are launched under such a system.

Technologies are developed for the purpose. This process keeps on going until desired improvement is achieved. As per requirement, this work is carried out at several places. For example the work of manufacturing of a satellite, a spacecraft, a missile etc. is carried out at several places simultaneously.

Question: Kindly state that in what manner and how the process of innovation is initiated?

Answer:

1. ***To identify the problem:*** The process of innovation is initiated by identifying the problem. It is identified only when a demand is raised.
2. ***To systemize the ideas:*** Under this head, several types of information and datas are required. Of them, certain information is easily available and efforts are made to secure other necessary information.
3. ***To find out a solution to the problem:*** Under this head, the information available is used in various ways. For this purpose, a new technique is developed or an existing technique is refined and adapted to resolve the problem.
4. ***To find a solution:*** One or more solutions are secured by making several types of experiments. The solution is not easily secured. It requires hard labour with dedication.
5. ***To test the solution:*** Under this process, more than one solutions are practically tested and if there is scope of such improvement as required, it is improved and is made economically viable. Further, it must examine whether it may be produced on a large scale or not.
6. ***To further share the knowledge after experiment:*** It is necessary for social progress.

The technology developed by an innovation may be helpful for other innovations. Thus, to make public, the knowledge acquired is not only in the interest of the society but the people conducting new experiment also get a base/ foundation.

Question: Are the innovators required in every field?

Answer: It has been observed that the innovators are required in every area/field. The current traditional methods and procedures in the offices in all our Government Departments need a change. Recently the Prime Minister has made an appeal to all the senior and superior officers that they should improve the efficiency in their respective offices through innovations. Innovations are also needed to help them to remove corruption from Govt. offices for obvious advantages.

Question: Have the utility and success of petty and ordinary innovations been assessed?

Answer: The survey conducted in this regard shows that the small innovations make simple changes in the function but they bring success in abundance.

Question: Has there been any survey conducted in the country that may indicate the percentage of small innovations?

Answer: According to a recently conducted survey, out of all the innovations so far made, the percentage of small and ordinary innovations is over 60%. Those small innovations have generally proved to be useful.

Question: Does the necessity of innovations depend upon the demand of market?

Answer: Necessity is the mother of innovation. Most of the innovations are prompted by necessities. Forty-five per cent innovations are based on market demand and 30% are made by effecting improvement during production process. Thus, nearly 75% innovations are demand-based because of the market requirements. Less than 25% are made by personal desire or due to personal initiative and the innovations so made are also significant.

Questions

1. How different types of innovations can be classified?
2. Does the process of innovation commence from identification of the problem? Please give example of 2/3 problems.
3. Whether Govt. functions or efficiency can be improved through innovations?
4. Can innovations help in reducing corruption in Govt. Offices?
5. Whether necessity is the mother of innovation/invention?

> *"Mere scientists are seldom great inventors. Innovations are usually produced by those who keep tinkering. Those who do not tinker almost never invent any thing new."*
>
> **—Prof. Yash Pal**

> *"Innovations never happen as planned."*
> **—Gifford Pinchot Quotes**

Points to Ponder

1. Please write, first of all, the gist of this chapter and thereafter answer each and every question clearly.
2. In case of any clarification, please do consult your mentor or write to the author of this book at the address given at the end of this book.
3. Suggestion, if any, to improve this chapter may please be sent to the author.

□

8

Nomenclature of an Innovation Product

> As parents have baptism of their children and masters of their domestic animals such as dogs and cats, an innovator has all rights to name his finished product after completion of the innovation. To give a proper name to an innovation is a vital function of an innovator.

Question: Please tell the significance of nomenclature of an innovative product?

Answer: An innovation, on being successful, is commercialized as a product. Therefore, its nomenclature becomes very important and significant. It should be so named that it reflects its properties and attract the consumers.

For an inventor, it becomes difficult to give a suitable name to his successful invention as the product has been invented for the first time. However, for an innovator this act is easier and simpler than an inventor.

Question: How and why is the nomenclature of an innovation product is necessary?

Answer: Ordinarily the object (Product) to be sold to consumers should be so named that the customer may easily understand what the object is and what its use is. For example, Amul Ice cream made by Amul Company. "Coca-Cola" where coca means tasteful leaf and cola means sweet carbonized drink. "Potato chips" means very thin layer i.e. a product made of potato. Similarly, "Pan Masala" and "Pan Bahar" etc. items provide information of their use by its very name. Thus, a number of names are found in the market which indicate as to what are the ingredients of that product.

Question: Please explain the answer of the above question in an easier manner so that all of us can understand it.

Answer: It is easier to give a name to a product, equipment, machine etc. after its successful innovation. By illustrating the process of selection of the names of the following two successful innovations, you would easily understand how those names were christened.

1. "Railway Ticket Dating Machine", after successful innovation, rechristened as "Self-Inking Railway Ticket Dating and Timing Machine", as it marks clearly on a ticket with black ink the date, month, year and time. Earlier the dates were pressed on card tickets which were not legible.
2. Hand Operated "Numbering Machine", prints only one line at a time and it was converted into a small printing machine, printing 3 or 4

lines at a stroke. It was rechristened as a "Micro Mini Printer". This clearly demonstrates that it is a very small printing device marking Batch No., Manufacturing date, Expiry date and MRP simultaneously on cartons, bags or any other objects in one stroke.

Question: Would it be proper for an innovator to discuss the nomenclature with his friend and colleagues?

Answer: The process of nomenclature is not very complicated but it is also not easy and simple. Therefore, an innovator must discuss the subject with his friends, colleagues, associates and co-workers and their suggestions should be taken into account. However, final decision to give name rests with the innovator himself.

Question: What tests should be passed by the nomenclature so that name of an innovative product is interesting and effective which may help in successful commercialization?

Answer: When the following three factors are satisfied, successful naming of an innovative product is probable.

1. Is the name of the product indicative of its use and working?
2. What image is created in the mind of people by hearing the name?
3. Is it easy to pronounce and remember the name?

Questions

1. Is the true – that the name of the product is helpful in its successful commercialization?

2. Whether name of the product should be short and simple so that it may be easily remembered by the customers?
3. Whether for a proper nomenclature of a product, the advice and consultation with family members, friends, associates etc. is proper?
4. Whether the name of the product demonstrates and indicates its properties and applications?

> *"It is better to have enough ideas for some of them to be wrong, than to be always right by having no ideas at all."*
>
> **—Edwar De Bono**

> *"A dream with courage is innovation ... A dream without courage is a delusion."*
>
> **—Anonymous**

Points to Ponder

1. Please write, first of all, the gist of this chapter and thereafter answer each and every question clearly.
2. In case of any clarification, please do consult your mentor or write to the author of this book at the address given at the end of this book.
3. Suggestion, if any, to improve this chapter may please be sent to the author.

□

9

Innovator's Diary

> To write a daily diary on fresh ideas occurring every day is an important aspect of life of an innovator. Sometimes such a diary or a note book becomes a matter of research. Thousands of pages of the notebook left by Thomas Alva Edison, the greatest inventor of 20th century, are read even today with inquisitiveness and several new inventions and innovations are coming up.

Question: Is it necessary for an innovator to always keep a diary or a notebook with him?

Answer: Every innovator should have a notebook which may easily be kept in his pocket and whenever a fresh idea occurs, it should be at once noted in the diary.

Question: Whether an innovator should record his efforts made from time-to-time in his diary?

Answer: He must note down his efforts whether his efforts are optimistic or pessimistic.

Question: Whether an innovator must go through his notebook from time-to-time?

Answer: For an innovator perusal of his diary or note-book from time-to-time may be useful because sometimes anything which appears to be odd or unreliable, it may afterwards be found logical. Sometimes odd and old ideas are also found to be more useful.

Question: Whether an innovator must note down date while writing his diary?

Answer: This habit may prove to be good and useful particularly when a dispute arises in securing a patent. When two innovators present their claims the date recorded in the diary becomes an important document at that time.

Question: Is it necessary to obtain signatures of a friend or colleague in the notebook?

Answer: In a dispute of securing patents the notebook which bears signatures of a reliable person or a friend with date, may prove to be much helpful.

Question: Is it necessary that every sheet of a note-book is numbered?

Answer: It is advisable that each and every page of a notebook should be numbered and no page is left un-numbered. It is not appropriate to remove a sheet from it.

Questions

1. Can you state that how keeping a diary be useful for an innovator?

2. What benefit other innovators can get by keeping such a diary?
3. Whether the old and odd ideas recorded in the diary may be helpful for an innovator in future?
4. Mainly what should be recorded in a diary by an innovator?

> *"Don't take rest after your first victory because if you fail in second, more lips are waiting to say that your first victory was just luck."*
>
> **—Prof. M.P. Varshney**

> *"Innovations are not the prerogative of some selected few. Even a person with no formal technical education can be innovative."*
>
> **—Prof. M.P. Varshney**

Points to Ponder

1. Please write, first of all, the gist of this chapter and thereafter answer each and every question clearly.
2. In case of any clarification, please do consult your mentor or write to the author of this book at the address given at the end of this book.
3. Suggestion, if any, to improve this chapter may please be sent to the author.

□

10

Benefits of Innovation

> Generally the society is benefitted from useful innovations. But their misuse generally proves to be painful, sad and disadvantageous.

Question: How the society is benefited from an innovation?

Answer: When production cost of a product is reduced through an innovation, its utility increases amongst consumers.

Question: How an innovation is useful for the society?

Answer: If risks are reduced by an innovation, its utility is enhanced in the society at large.

Question: Whether innovation improves the standard of living?

Answer: Yes, standard of living is generally improved. Innovation of products like mixer, washing machine, cooking gas and cooker have brought rapid improvements in operation and has made life easy and comfortable.

Question: Whether the efficiency is improved by innovation?

Answer: Efficiency and functioning are improving rapidly as a result of innovations made in the field of communication, mobile phone, computer and internet.

Question: What is the contribution of innovations in the development of a nation?

Answer: The countries where innovative culture is speedily growing and are producing and bringing new products and equipments in the market by updating them quickly. In this direction Japan, America and Germany are much ahead of other countries. By rapid economic growth, these countries have become rich and prosperous.

Question: What benefit does an innovator get from innovation?

Answer: A successful innovator gets self-satisfaction as also self-confidence for his works. He further feels pleasure, joy and delight.

Question: Whether an innovator gains financial benefits?

Answer: Of course, after successful commercialization of an innovation, the innovator gains financial benefits and many innovators become rich within a short period of time. Several successful innovators became multimillionaires by means of innovation. We all are aware that Bill Gates has become one of the richest persons of the world with innovations related to the computers. He is reckoned as the biggest donor in the world.

Question: What other benefits are gained by an innovator in addition to the financial gains and benefits?

Answer: A successful innovator gains social recognition in addition to the respect and honour. Many successful innovators are granted recognition at international level apart from the national level, only if the utility of those innovations is recognized internationally.

Question: Whether other people of society get encouraged by the inspiring acts of the innovators?

Answer: The persons of positive thinking are definitely impressed by the inspiring acts of others and they too venture to proceed on that path.

Question: How do the family members of an innovator evaluate him?

Answer: This issue is in fact very tricky. Therefore, it cannot be answered easily. Many family members term the innovator as a crazy, certain people term him as a man of unsound mind and others call him as a mad person. Further, there are people who say that he is wasting time in unnecessary activities. Of course, there are very few people who have positive thoughts in respect to the innovator. A true innovator is a person who is deeply involved in his act unmindful of such ideas and conjectures.

Questions

1. How is the society and nation benefited by an innovation?

2. Whether innovations provide vital contribution to the security of the country?
3. Whether a successful innovator may become a source of inspiration to others?
4. Whether a successful innovator acquires a special position in the society and how does he gains respect and honour as well as dignity?
5. How people evaluate an innovator at the initial stages?

> *"Every organization-not just business-needs one core competence! Innovation."*
>
> **—Peter F. Drucker**

Points to Ponder

1. Please write, first of all, the gist of this chapter and thereafter answer each and every question clearly.
2. In case of any clarification, please do consult your mentor or write to the author of this book at the address given at the end of this book.
3. Suggestion, if any, to improve this chapter may please be sent to the author.

□

11
Innovation Workshop

Every work requires a proper place and congenial environment which have vital impact on the speed and quality of the work. In the beginning an innovator alone starts working in his small room or garage. It appears to be a strong coincidence that the word "Karkhana" in Hindi (i.e. factory) might have been coined from the word Kar-khana (garage). Many big inventions and innovations were started from a garage. Steve Jobs, a co-founder of Apple Computers, a great visionary, creative genius and innovator, started his innovative works from his garage.

Question: Whether large sites or workshops required for minor/small inventions/innovations?

Answer: To begin with no large sites or workshops are required for minor / small innovations. They may be performed at small type of small places as farm, threshing fields, kitchen, bathroom, bedroom, guestroom and garden etc. They may also happen in small offices and small workshops.

Question: Is seclusion necessary for an innovator?

Answer: A true innovator is constant thinker and therefore he needs solitude. It is in his interest to keep away from noise. If his activity is hampered, his mind would be disturbed and he may not be able to concentrate on his work and deviate from his path. Therefore, he needs a complete solitude and concentration.

Question: What type of materials/equipments required by an innovator for learning and finding solution to problems?

Answer: For learning, the innovator requires books, manuals and catalogues. He also needs equipments and tools for trial and conduct of experiments.

Question: How an innovator is benefitted by today's modern amenities, equipments such as computer, internet and scanner?

Answer: These amenities are very vital for his learning and enhancing his knowledge. The innovator may learn a lot provided he is fully computer literate.

Question: What does innovator expects from his family members, parents, siblings, wife, teachers and neighbours?

Answer: The innovator expects good wishes, good behaviour, cooperation and if required, petty assistance from members of his family, neighbourers and teachers. The peaceful atmosphere set up by them does support him in nurturing of the process of innovation.

Question: Please tell us what type of a workshop is required by an ordinary innovator for minor and small innovations, and what type of equipments is needed by him?

Answer: To begin with, a new innovator should make efforts to mobilize necessary equipments from here and there for want of money and thus he should set up his laboratory. The need is that minimum amount of money is spent on tools and equipments and the utmost endeavour should be to mobilize the things from his family, friends and neighbourers. There is no option except to purchase rest of the things from market.

An innovator needs following things for his attempt to make a new or novel product in his workshop:

1. The laboratory, even if small one, must be neat and clean.
2. For the purpose of his activity, a bench, light provision on the bench and stool for sitting should be there.
3. The provision of keeping things-used card boards, plastic, wooden boxes and tin boxes may be used for this purpose.
4. Equipments, tools, screwdriver, hammer, pliers, twister, scissors, scale, drill, measuring ribbon, bit for drill, clamp, knife, small raw, file and sand paper.
5. Screw, rubber tape, thin wires, gum, other adhesive liquid as araldite, nails, ropes, wood pieces, electronics parts, plastic parts, rubber parts and metal components.

6. Useless domestic items that may be used in innovations, making models such as cardboard, used tins, wire, papers, paper clips, matchboxes and aluminium blades.
7. Several domestic equipments which are redundant may be used in the process of invention and innovation. Used radio parts, tape recorder, toys, locks, camera, lamp, typewriter, cycle and telephone, many times their parts may be removed and are used to make a model.

Question: Is it practicable to do big and complex innovations in such small workshops?

Answer: It is not possible to do big and complex innovations in small workshops. Very big and well equipped and well managed workshops are required for large and complex innovations where several innovators and inventors may work jointly on different projects. It takes years and incurs huge expenditure on successful development of a new product as well as on effective marketing of a newly developed complex innovative product. However, on successful commercialization of the product, the innovation becomes a great source of huge earnings.

Questions

1. Whether a workshop is necessary for small, medium and large innovations?
2. Is it practicable to undertake innovations at the places other than the workshops? If, yes, state

one or two places where successful innovations have been undertaken?

3. Is it possible to perform innovation without modern amenities such as computer, internet etc?
4. What articles and equipments are required in a good and a well managed small laboratory? Please state name of ten articles and equipments.

"Today, we have confidence in building the new innovative India of our dreams as is evident from our major successes in the arena of many technological innovations which have made such a difference to the nation, including the blue (space), green (agriculture), white (milk), and gray (software) revolutions. Also, India has major strengths in technological innovation on the human front in terms of the largest pool of qualified engineers in the world and the seventh largest pool of R&D personnel and on the institutional front in terms of impressive array of research centres and laboratories, and a host of so-called traditional technologies. A majority of the Fortune five hundred Companies considers India as the preferred destination for locating their innovation centres. It is a very appropriate time to strengthen our efforts in reviving India's creativity and innovative spirit as a national movement today."

—Dr. R.A. Mashelkar

Points to Ponder

1. Please write, first of all, the gist of this chapter and thereafter answer each and every question clearly.
2. In case of any clarification, please do consult your mentor or write to the author of this book at the address given at the end of this book.
3. Suggestion, if any, to improve this chapter may please be sent to the author.

□

12

Manufacture of Sale of Innovated Product

> Considerable time, money and energy are invested in the manufacture of a product. Conduct of an innovation is a different type of activity but manufacture of the product based on the innovation is a different type of activity.

Question: Whether a product based on a small innovation should be manufactured by innovator himself?

Answer: For this purpose money and resources are required. Therefore, for a small innovator, it is not without risk to manufacture it himself as several types of hardships and hurdles may come in way of manufacturing.

Question: What type of hardships and hurdles arise in self-manufacturing?

Answer: First of all a workshop, money, machine and energy are required. Then several types of instruments and equipments as well as efficient artisan are required.

Question: Whether a product may be manufactured on a small scale?

Answer: If the product of an innovator is simple, it is easy and less expensive to manufacture it on small scale. To start with such a product may be manufactured and sold on experimental basis. Thus, the innovator would come to know whether his product would be acceptable in the market or not.

Question: Whether an innovator can decide to commercialize the product on large scale after it is accepted in the market?

Answer: For a small innovator, it is not so easy to manufacture it on a large scale and then carry on business because a lot of resources and means are required for that.

Question: Please state how can a product be manufactured on large scale and demand of the market is met?

Answer: In case the product is found to be a very useful for the society, any big manufacturer may be willing to enter into an agreement with innovator on the terms and conditions mutually settled.

Question: Can the patent or design of innovation be sold to a manufacturer?

Answer: Generally innovations are sold by two modes:

1. The manufacturer pays the amount in lump sum to the innovator and gets all the rights of

manufacturing and sale. Thereafter, the innovator ceases to have any rights to it.

2. The manufacturer secures right to manufacture it only. But the innovator gets royalty on the sale of the product under the agreement.

Question: What precautions an innovator has to exercise with the manufacturer?

Answer: Ordinarily an innovator has to keep in mind three types of precautions as follows:

1. To select an appropriate manufacturing company.
2. To present his innovation properly before the manufacturing company.
3. To enter into a lawful and profitable agreement with the manufacturing company.

Question: How is the retail price of a product based on the innovation fixed?

Answer: If your product is found more useful and better in quality than other products available in the market, its retail price may be fixed a little higher. If product has no competitor in the market, it is easier to fix the retail price with higher amount of profit. It fetches more financial gains to the innovator as well as manufacturing Company.

Question: Is it necessary for an innovator and a manufacturer to know about the reaction of consumers?

Answer: In the age of severe competition, it is very necessary to seek reactions of consumers. It is advisable that the innovator should continue to improve his product. It would be advantageous to have feedback from market from time-to-time so that the innovator may bring necessary alterations in the product and make more simple and useful. In case, both innovator and the manufacturer have cordial relations between them, it would be profitable not only to both of them but the society at large, would the benefitted.

Questions

1. What resources are required for the manufacturing of a product based on the innovation?
2. What precautions are required by a small innovator in manufacturing his product himself?
3. Whether a product should be manufactured on large scale only after it is accepted in the market? Write the manner in which market acceptance may be secured.
4. By which method an innovator can fix retail price of his product?
5. What precautions should be exercised by him, while fixing the retail price?
6. How a product may be launched successfully in the market?

> *"Without your involvement you can't succeed. With your involvement you can't fail."*
>
> **—Dr. A.P.J. Abdul Kalam**

> *"Today, need for an innovation movement is of paramount importance, as we have come to a juncture where economic independence is to be achieved through innovating India. Innovations are lifelines for industry or business house."*
>
> **—Prof. Murli Manohar Joshi**

Points to Ponder

1. Please write, first of all, the gist of this chapter and thereafter answer each and every question clearly.
2. In case of any clarification, please do consult your mentor or write to the author of this book at the address given at the end of this book.
3. Suggestion, if any, to improve this chapter may please be sent to the author.

□

13

Information About Patents

> An innovation is very precious achievement. There is always a fear that someone else may not steal and copy it and establish his industry thereby becoming a competitor. Thus, the poor real innovator loses all advantages.

Question: Whether the procedure of patents must be brought to the notice of small innovators?

Answer: It is absolutely necessary that name of the innovator is affixed with the innovation. Therefore, it is a vital and important issue that the innovator must secure information about patent law. There should not be any relaxation in this matter.

Question: Whether a small innovator should get his innovation patented?

Answer: An innovator applies his skill, imagination, labour and resources for conduct of an innovation and making a useful product. It is necessary to seek grant of patent for his product. It becomes therefore the duty and responsibility of the government in public interest to provide security to the innovator so that competitors may not cause any harm to him.

Question: What benefit would an innovator get by Patent?

Answer: By means of a patent an agreement between an innovator and the Government is considered to the effect that the innovator would show his acquired knowledge and on the basis of the acquired knowledge the innovator would get adequate benefit of the innovation for a certain period of time.

Question: Whether all innovations may be granted patent?

Answer: No. If that type of innovation has been granted patent earlier, the current innovation cannot be granted patent. Therefore, before applying for grant of a patent it is necessary to know that whether the kind of innovation conducted by you has already been made/done or not and whether right of patent has been granted to that innovator.

Question: Whether small innovators need help from Patent Attorneys?

Answer: The patent procedure being complicated, for small innovators it is not only necessary to seek the assistance of Patent Attorney but it is essential too. A good reliable Patent Attorney can assist you in all respects.

Question: How can we know whether our innovation is new one or not?

Answer: The Patent Office maintains all past information related to Patents in the classified form. The innovator may obtain necessary information from there. The innovator has to do the search work himself also.

Question: I have started making use of my innovation. I have been selling a product based on it for two years. Can I now apply for a Patent?

Answer: Ordinarily, no application can be moved for a patent of an item in use or in operation for the period of over one year, i.e. after a stipulated period.

Question: I published the details of my innovation in an article in a journal about one and half year ago. Can I now apply for grant of Patent of the innovation?

Answer: In case of an object already made public before a stipulated period, no application for its Patent can be moved. The article should be published in journal only after an application for a patent has been filed with Patent Office.

Question: In case two people separately apply for a Patent of the same thing what would happen?

Answer: In such a case the Patent Office would decide whose claim is genuine and who has conducted the innovation earlier and independently. Here comes the importance of keeping a notebook.

Question: Does the Patent Office assist in developing and selling an innovation?

Answer: No. Under the guidelines, the officers and staff of the patents office have to maintain complete secrecy till publication of advertisement on a patent.

Question: Whether the right to an innovation may be partly or wholly sold after the application for a patent has been filed?

Answer: Yes. The innovator may sell his rights partially or wholly.

Question: What action is taken by the patents office if another person uses the innovation an unauthorized manner despite the fact that the patent has already been granted?

Answer: It is your duty to secure your patent. The patents office simply grants patents. If it is violated the patents office takes no action. It is your responsibility that you initiate a legal action or file a case against him in the court of law.

Question: Whether an attorney can transfer or pass on the information of an innovation to another person? If he does so, what action may be taken against him?

Answer: Generally the professional attorneys do not indulge in such things as they get defamed by doing so and their legal practice is affected. In case an attorney does so, his complaint can be lodged with the concerned authorities and his practice may be banned.

Question: Where the Head Office of Patent Law is located?

Answer: Presently, a patent is granted under the Patent Act 1970 of the Govt. of India and the procedure of Patent is followed under the Rules of 1972. The Head

Office of Patent is located in Kolkata and its branch offices are situated in Delhi, Mumbai, and Chennai.

Questions

1. Is it necessary to seek grant of a patent of every innovation?
2. What benefit the innovator gets by grant of a patent?
3. Whether patent may be granted for all innovations?
4. Whether publication of an article or allowing interview on his product may be harmful for an innovator?
5. Whether the patents office may give some assistance to the innovator in case of the violation of a patent?

> *"Let us today pledge to make India a great power in Science and Technology. This is essential for the realization of the higher goal we have set for ourselves: To make the 21st Century India's century-**Ikkeesveen Shatabdi Bharat Ki Shatabdi**".*
>
> *Make science and scientific temper an integral part of national life and launch an "Innovation Movement."*
>
> **—Atal Bihari Vajpayee**

Points to Ponder

1. Please write, first of all, the gist of this chapter

and thereafter answer each and every question clearly.

2. In case of any clarification, please do consult your mentor or write to the author of this book at the address given at the end of this book.
3. Suggestion, if any, to improve this chapter may please be sent to the author.

□

14

Awards and Honours

In all communities of the world- big and small, whenever a person does a new/novel and good work in the interest of the society, he is recognized by the society in different ways. Such a person acquires a distinct identity in the society. Such recognition encourages him to do more good works.

Question: Please state how small and ordinary innovators are encouraged in our country?

Answer: There are some government and non-government organizations in the country which encourage small innovators for good work but number of such institutions is very limited. Therefore, it is necessary that the people should come forward to encourage small innovators. The National Innovation Foundation, Innovation Forum, Sristi Innovations are the institutions working in this field.

Question: Whether the State governments have framed any special scheme to award honours to small and ordinary innovators?

Answer: None of the State Government has so far framed any scheme separately to felicitate small innovators only. However, under general scheme of Awards and Honours of the State Governments small innovators are selected for awards after their work has been evaluated. Such a state of affairs is not justified. There should be separate scheme for Awards for small/grassroot innovators.

Question: Whether the Government of India or its Ministries have framed any special scheme to felicitate small and ordinary innovators?

Answer: No Ministry of the Government of India has framed any such scheme so far to encourage the small innovators individually by way of giving awards and honours. They are selected under general scheme which is not a healthy tradition to encourage small innovators to compete with big innovators.

Question: Whether Government of India has launched any scheme to recognize and to felicitate with awards for contributing excellent traditional knowledge?

Answer: In the year 2000, the Government of India had set up the National Innovation Foundation with the primary objective to recognize and give awards and honours for innovation made by creative people of village, town, urban poor clusters and the persons contributing excellent traditional knowledge. In fact this scheme is encouragement for small and grass root innovators. All state Governments must set up such organizations to encourage the innovators doing excellent work in their states. The people making innovations based on traditional knowledge may also be given proper recognition and award.

Question: Would you please state when and how should the awards and honours be given?

Answer: An innovation should be evaluated properly at a proper time so that the awards are given adequately and also on time. The honour should be accompanied by a proper cash award then only other people of the society particularly youth, who are fleeing from science today would get attracted to it. The series of award should start from the district level and go up to the national level. Then only students and ordinary people would join the process of innovation.

Question: Whether big industrial houses have launched any award scheme in this sphere?

Answer: So far the big business houses in India have not paid any serious attention to it. However, they encourage their workmen in different ways for their novel works and give them cash awards. Recently MERICO Innovation Foundation, Mumbai has laid down a scheme of awards in four different fields i.e. social, vocational, business for social innovation and innovations in public sector under which "Innovation India Awards", are given every year.

Question: Whether social organizations and educational institutions also inspire small innovators for their excellent performance by way of giving awards?

Answer: None of the big social organization at national level has come forward so far to frame any such scheme. However, one or two social organizations at local level do felicitate and give awards to innovators. Such social organizations include Rotary Club, Bharat Vikas Parishad etc.

Question: Are innovators encouraged by big industrial houses, social and educational institutions to make innovations in the foreign countries?

Answer: To my knowledge, in America, nearly 34 small and big non-government institutions and organizations are providing incentives to students and ordinary innovators under various schemes for many years. Various schemes of incentives are as follows: To give cash awards, commendation letters, free visit to Research Institutes and Science Museums, to encourage students in vacations to take part in various innovative activities by inviting them to the camps. The institutions bear all the expenses of such camps. Such various non-government organizations and institutions have been functioning in other western countries too for many years.

Question: Why are such activities not organized in our country?

Answer: We have not yet identified economic and social significance of innovations. Therefore, we have not progressed or made any headway in this field. For last ten years certain activities have, however, taken place in this area which need to be accelerated. Industrial and business houses must come forward to make headway in this important area for economic development and social change.

Questions

1. Do the awards and honours prompt the innovators?
2. Do the awards prompt other people of the society?
3. Is it proper to recognize successful innovators at school and college level?
4. Would it be proper for local industrial units/ social organizations to felicitate successful innovators?
5. Whether an award scheme, to encourage innovators, should be launched at Tehsil, District, Division, State and National Level?
6. How big industrial organizations and social institutions can play an important role in promoting innovations in their areas?

> *"Knowledge and Wisdom are to be converted into wealth for better India. More and more inventors have now started realizing that* ***LAKSHMI Tab Aayangee Jab SARASWATI Muskarayangee.*** *In other words, innovative idea is key for economic prosperity."*
>
> **—Dr. R.A. Mashelkar**

Points to Ponder

1. Please write, first of all, the gist of this chapter

and thereafter answer each and every question clearly.

2. In case of any clarification, please do consult your mentor or write to the author of this book at the address given at the end of this book.
3. Suggestion, if any, to improve this chapter may please be sent to the author.

□

15

The Innovator-Elevated to the Highest Office

The citizens doing good and novel work get a distinct position in the society. They are honoured by the society in different forms. In every country, the scientists, inventors and innovators are appointed to the posts under Government Departments and Non-Government Organizations (N.G.Os) on the basis of their qualifications, experience and achievements . Such persons are elevated to the highest office of the country for their exceptional contributions and achievements.

Question: Can you kindly tell us about the scientists, inventors and innovators of the country who have occupied the highest offices and received highest civilian awards.

Answer: There are several eminent scientists like Professor Yash Pal, Dr. R.A. Mashelkar, Dr. K. Kasturirangan, Dr. M.S. Swaminathan, Prof.

M.G.K. Menon, Dr. R. Chidambaram etc. who were appointed as Secretary of different Scientific Departments of the Government of India and also each of them were honoured with one of the highest civilian awards, "Padma Vibhushan".

Question: Whether the highest Civilian Award of the country has been given to a scientist, inventor and innovator in India?

Answer: Dr. A.P.J. Abdul Kalam was an eminent scientist as well as a great innovator. He was a scientist and innovator who was awarded 'Bharat Ratna', by the Government of India after C.V. Raman (1954) for his exceptional work in 1997. Besides, Dr. C.V. Raman and Dr. A.P.J. Abdul Kalam, another renowned scientist Dr. C.N.R. Rao was also honoured with 'Bharat Ratna Award' in 2013.

Question: Whether any scientist, inventor or an innovator has been elevated to the post of President of India?

Answer: In the year 2002, Dr. A.P.J. Abdul Kalam was elected as President of India. He was a very active President and will always be remembered as a successful and people's President.

Question: Please state some important social innovations made by Dr. Kalam?

Answer: Dr. Kalam has made a number of significant innovations in the area of national security. The successful manufacturing of "Artificial Limbs", for physically challenged people from a light substance developed for satellite and a pacemaker

"Kalam-Raju Stunt", for a very low price in the area of health care are his two noted socially useful innovations.

Question: Whether the inventors and innovators in foreign countries have been given an opportunity to be elevated to the highest office of the country?

Answer: Nearly 250 years ago George Washington, the first President of U.S.A., was an inventor and innovator. He innovated a novel type of plough. The second plough made by him was such a modified version that sowing could be carried along with the plough. He invented a basket for putting liquor bottles that could be easily revolved on the dinner table.

Abraham Lincoln was considered to be one of the most popular and progressive Presidents of U.S.A. He was also a successful innovator. His Home Secretary, Thomas Jefferson, who became the President later, was also a successful inventor and innovator.

Question: Is there any scientist who turned down the offer of the office of President?

Answer: When Israel became a new nation, the greatest scientist of 20th century Albert Einstein, who had a great impact on the whole world, was approached to grace the office of President of Israel. But he turned down the offer with humility. He wanted to remain awfully preoccupied in his scientific pursuits and had no interest in the office of a President. In fact, it is an example to be remembered and quoted forever in future throughout the world.

Questions

1. Can you state the names of two U.S. Presidents who performed successful innovations?
2. Can you state something about two socially useful innovations made by Dr. Kalam? What type of people are being benefitted from them?
3. Is there a scientist in the world who has turned down the offer of the office of President?
4. State one or two Indian Innovators or Scientists who have worked on highest posts in various departments of the Government of India.

> *"When a nation recognizes the innovators, the nation gets intellectually elevated. It is very much necessary to keep the minds ignited and the process intact."*
>
> **—Dr. A.P.J. Abdul Kalam**

> *"We can win future by promoting innovations which will bring economic prosperity."*
>
> **—Bill Gates**

Points to Ponder

1. Please write, first of all, the gist of this chapter and thereafter answer each and every question clearly.
2. In case of any clarification, please do consult your mentor or write to the author of this book at the address given at the end of this book.
3. Suggestion, if any, to improve this chapter may please be sent to the author.

□

16
Innovators Multimillionaires and Philanthropist

These days the students generally think that scientists, inventors and innovators have their roles in laboratories only. But it is not true. Progress of scientists, inventors and innovators, doing work useful for society, has no limits. There are several inventors and innovators who became millionaire and multi-millionaires with their ordinary and simple inventions or innovations.

There are historical proofs that the persons, who were never science students, made simple and ordinary inventions and innovations to satisfy the petty needs of people and society thereby earned huge amount of money. A large portion of that wealth was spent by them for promotion of education and social welfare activities and thus they become immortal among people.

Question: Please state the names and works of certain innovators who became multimillionaires within a short period and then made good use of the money in philanthropic activities?

Answer: Many big and small innovations have occurred in U.S.A. However, it would be more useful to state about certain small innovators who became millionaires.

1. In 1952, Beta Nesmith, a typist in U.S.A., innovated and manufactured a fluid, similar to the white nail polish, for the purpose of rubbing and correcting typing errors. The demand was so widespread in the whole world that it became popular by the name of *"Correction Fluid"*. In the year 1976, 25 million bottles of correction fluid were sold all over the world. Unfortunately, the lady died in the year 1979 at the age of 55. She left the property worth 5 crores US dollars. As per her Will, its half share i.e. 2.5 crores US dollars went to her only son and remaining sum of 2.5 crores US dollars was donated for social and charitable activities.
2. After the second world war was over in 1945, Navyman Edward Lave, on retirement from U.S. Navy, started the business of Wooden Powder which was used for absorbing oil and grease. However, as it was flammable, he developed a new substance which proved to be very useful for cat cages in comparison to the use in factories. He named it *"Kitty Litter"*,

which became useful for putting in the cat cages. It would keep the cage dry and therefore its demand increased year by year. Eventually, Edward Lave earned a huge wealth by this small product. He founded Training Institute, in order to support the small entrepreneurs, on the land of 3000 acres in Michigan State investing a huge capital of 3 crores US dollars. Lave authored books as well as Directories for use of Traders. Before his death in the year 1990, he sold out his company for the sum of 20 crores US dollars.

3. An ordinary motor mechanic Natte Sherman started the business of spareparts of cars in 1940. He prepared a multilayer unrusted *Muffler* (Silencer). After polishing it was shining like gold and his business spread in several cities of U.S.A. In 1993, its turnover reached 100 crores US dollars. With the money so earned Sherman established Midas Institute of Technology (M.I.T.). He was a fast friend of Israel. He used to donate huge amounts for the welfare of Jews. He was confidential and financial advisor to the then Prime Minister Golda Meir.
4. In the year 1853, Levi Strauss at the age of 24, who had shifted to U.S.A. from Europe, 6 years after, started making pants from thick canvas cloth. They were found very useful for labourers/workers. It is now known by name

of *"Jeans"*, throughout the world. Levi Strauss substituted a twilled cotton cloth from France called "serge de nimes." The fabric later became known as denim and the pants were nicknamed blue jeans. The company earned the profit to the tune of 24 lakh US dollars by 1880. He gave free of cost 18,000 company shares to his employees. The enthusiastic employees expanded the business very rapidly. With the increasing business his profit also went up quickly. Well off and rich Strauss donated the money for several types of religious activities. He also launched a scheme of scholarship for deaf and dumb students in the University of California.

Even after the death of Levi Strauss in 1902, his successors continued to donate huge amounts for religious activities.

Question: Please state about some Indian Innovators who supported and promoted the philanthropic activities.

Answer: In India, there are a number of such innovators.

1. These days the use of powder of spices packed in paperboxes is rapidly increasing in big cities and towns. Such an innovative scheme was first launched nearly 50 years ago by Mahashaya Dharma Pal. His business of spices gradually increased and is today known as M.D.H. spices in India and abroad. He is now known and

recognized as 'King of Spices'. Thus, Mahashaya Dharma Pal not only became an arabpati but he acquired huge properties as well. He gives lakhs of rupees in charity every year to several social and religious organizations. He has been patron and president of several social organizations. He founded in Delhi a very big 300 bed hospital known an, "Mata Chanan Devi Hospital". It is equipped with all types of modern amenities and machines where the beneficiaries are the people belonging to lower strata of society. In addition, he is habitual of giving financial support to the poor and no poor would go empty-handed from his house or factory. Further, he appears himself and acts interestingly in the advertisements of his products on T.V. There is no other *crorepati* or *arabpati* in India who is engaged personally in giving the publicity of his products through TV. It is in itself a wonderful innovation.

2. The price of washing soaps manufactured by multi-national companies was so high that it was beyond the reach of common and poor people in India. Keeping in view this requirement, Karsan Bhai Patel from Gujarat gave a deep thought to this problem nearly 40 years ago and he innovated and manufactured *"Nirma"*, washing soap which has given poor a great relief. He started this business with a

single worker and today nearly 40 thousand workers are engaged in the manufacturing activities and the annual business of Nirma Soap is estimated over Rs. 2500 crores. Today this soap has become very popular in small villages and towns.

Karsan Bhai Patel, the innovator of this soap, has established a big university in Gujarat in order to promote education and has done a commendable work thereby. He has been giving financial support to several social institutions time-to-time. He is always ready to help the poor and pitiable with open mind. Karsan Bhai has been awarded several awards and honours. Further two universities of U.S. have awarded Honorary Degree of Doctorate to him.

A petty innovative idea did make Karsan Bhai not only a *crorepati* but inspired him to do praiseworthy work in the fields of social service and education.

3. The author of this book, Lakshman Prasad has made about 25 innovations within last 30 years of which 12 innovations have been successfully commerciali-zed. With the financial gain accrued from the business, he established in 1995 a *"Viklang Kalyan Kendra"*, in the City of Aligarh for providing artificial limbs free of cost to the physically challenged and also financially supported the establishment of a mentally

challenged children school in Lucknow.

He provided a huge monetary support in the establishment of a Model Rural Education Institution namely *"C.B. Gupta Saraswati Vidyapeeth"*, Village Singharpur, District Aligarh for the students of rural areas. Further, he has been providing financial assistance to several social activities from time-to-time in order to promote them.

Lakshman Prasad has initiated to celebrate *National Innovation Day,* in the country from year 2000 in order to promote innovative culture in the country. Innovation Day is celebrated on 15th Oct. every year in several schools, colleges, universities etc. of the country. He provides financial assistance to some schools and colleges also. With his inspiration, the *International Innovation Day*, is being celebrated from 2006 on a large scale on 15th October every year at International Level under the leadership of Shrimati and Dr. Jagdish Gandhi, Founder of C.M.S., Lucknow, the biggest educational institute in the world. Thousands of students from several countries participate properly voluntarily in the various activities organized on International Innovation Day every year.

He has published 13 books on Innovation and Invention to give impetus to foster innovative culture in the country for the last 20 years.

As a successful innovator, he has been giving lectures and interacting with students of highly reputed educational institutions like IIMs, IITs, engineering and management colleges, several P.G. colleges, universities and renowned business schools of the country on different aspects of the subject of innovation. He does not accept any honorarium for his lecturers and talks from these institutions. Over one lakh students have been benefitted by his talks.

Questions

1. Does every successful innovator have a dream to become a *crorepati*?
2. Can you please state about the works of one or two small successful innovators abroad who became *crorepati*?
3. How did Mahashaya Dharmpal became a *crorepati* as well as a successful innovator?
4. With what particular objectives did Dr. Jagdish Gandhi start holding International Innovation Day? What benefit is his organization getting thereby?

> *"Innovation distinguishes between a leader and a follower."*
>
> **—Steve Jobs**

> *"Creative ideas are much more powerful than several atom bombs; they are much more superior than several super computers and they can travel much faster than the speed of many supersonic aircrafts."*
>
> **—Lakshman Prasad**

Points to Ponder

1. Please write, first of all, the gist of this chapter and thereafter answer each and every question clearly.
2. In case of any clarification, please do consult your mentor or write to the author of this book at the address given at the end of this book.
3. Suggestion, if any, to improve this chapter may please be sent to the author.

□

17
Collection of Creative Ideas

Creative ideas have in fact vital role to play in building a new society through process of innovations. The building of a new society is not possible without it. In the whole world technological changes are taking place very rapidly. This age has given a slogan, "innovate or perish". In fact those countries have a future that can compete successfully in the race of technological innovations. The technical innovations cannot resolve not only the problems arising before the country but may contribute much more significantly in the economic development . Therefore, our country very much needs new creative ideas for technological innovations.

Question: How do the creative ideas occur?

Answer: Creativity comes from within and flows out wards for the benefit of the society.

Question: Do the creative ideas arise in the mind of a particular person or group of persons?

Answer: It would not be proper to claim that creative ideas arise in the minds of educated and experienced persons only. Such ideas arise in the minds of all classes of persons as men and women, educated and illiterate, children and youth, youngsters and aged, scientists and technocrats, physically challenged and normal persons from time-to-time. Ordinarily these ideas vanish or forgotten after lapse of time. Eventually, many good ideas are lost if not properly used by converting them into useful innovations (products).

Question: Is there any scheme by which good substantive and constructive ideas may be collected for a longer period of time?

Answer: If these ideas are efficiently and effectively collected, they would not vanish and may sooner or later be translated into action in public interest. This process may be possible only when a bank of creative ideas is set up.

Question: Why have the banks of creative ideas not set up so far? How and then to whom did this idea occur?

Answer: The idea of setting up the banks of creative ideas first of all occurred in the mind of Lakshman Prasad, the author of this book, when he was delivering a lecture on innovation before the learned faculty of the world renowned management institute-IIM, Ahmedabad in October 1999. Almost all the faculty members not only welcome this idea but strongly supported the idea of setting up such banks in India.

Question: What are the views of great scientists of the country, teachers and directors of higher technology institutes on the subject?

Answer: A number of eminent scientists like Missileman Dr. A.P.J. Abdul Kalam, Prof. Yash Pal, Dr. R.A. Mashelkar, Prof. V. Ramamurthy, Prof. S.K.Guha, Dr. K. Kasturirangan etc. and several senior faculty and directors of Indian Institutes of Management and Indian Institutes of Technology, have expressed their appreciation for this initiative. Besides, Naresh Chandra, Former Cabinet Secretary and Ambassador of India to USA, Girish Chandra Saxena, Former Governor of Jammu and Kashmir and Former Comptroller and Auditor General of India, Gian Prakash have also expressed their views in its support.

Question: Please state what type of persons would be especially benefitted by establishment of such banks.

Answer: This question is in fact very important. It has been noticed that there are some people who have very good substantive and constructive ideas but they are unable to translate the same into innovations as necessary facilities or infrastructure or technical support/assistance are not available to them. Therefore, such good ideas remain un-used and unutilized. It has been further noticed that some talented persons have knack of converting ideas into innovation. But sometimes unfortunately, they are found as struggling for creative ideas to utilize their skill and innovative techniques. Therefore, it was felt that some agency is established which could collect ideas from different people and from different parts of the country and pool them at one place. Those, who are in need of creative ideas for making innovations and inventions, may obtain or borrow the ideas from the above agency.

Question: Will you please tell the primary objective of the proposed bank and how would it operate?

Answer: Main objectives of the proposed bank:

The main objective of creating the Bank of Creative Ideas is to help individuals to promote inventions and innovations. This will also help to hasten the process of making India inventive and innovative in meeting challenges of high magnitude, arising out of a multitude of problems including population explosion.

The functions of the Bank are envisaged as under:

(a) To create environment for the development of creative ideas by motivational campaigns.

(b) To solicit ideas from all parts of the country and register only feasible and viable ideas after proper scrutiny.

(c) To pool such ideas and make their proper classification.

(d) To supply the ideas required by an individual or an organization interested in converting them into inventions and innovations.

(e) To identify individuals or organizations who can transform the innovations into products or utilities.

(f) To carry out other functions assigned in the fulfillment of the objectives of the bank.

The functions of the bank, as visualized above, may then be expanded according to the needs of different innovators, inventors and institutions.

Question: What type of precautions are required in establishment of the proposed bank?

Answer: After constitution of a bank once, its scope may be further extended. It is a matter of great importance that proper secrecy must be kept and exercised in exchange of creative ideas. Further the persons giving potential ideas should be honoured and monetarily rewarded. They should be given the share of profits earned in case his idea is successfully implemented. Further, the person implementing these ideas, should be provided with necessary technical and financial assistance as well. If the person or organization receiving the idea has entered into an agreement with the bank that whenever the product based on the idea is commercially successful, the bank should also get the share of profits. It would further enhance the importance of that bank.

Question: What type of persons are required to operate the bank smoothly?

Answer: In order to operate the bank smoothly and efficiently, the persons well versed with advance technical know-how and possessing technical and managerial qualifications would be required. Integrity of highest order would be an important requisite. No individual can start such type of bank. This work can be started by a competent organization possessing financial resources as well as legal authority.

Question: Is this a Crazy Idea?

Answer: No. Today the idea of a bank may appear to be imaginary but that day is not far away when such banks would not only come into existence in various countries but would play effective role in solving various challenges. It may be pointed out in this regard that some industrial houses in India i.e. Times of India Group, Mahindras have recently started inviting constructive ideas relating to the industry through big advertisements in important news-papers. They have also announced cash prizes and incentives for useful industrial ideas. Similarly, a social organization from Singapore has also launched a massive campaign to compile the socially creative ideas through newspapers. It has announced to honour those providing useful social innovative ideas.

It is a misfortune of our country and it has become our mentality that we do not recognize the original novel ideas or products produced in our country unless they were recognized and accepted in western countries. This situation is regrettable.

Question: Whether compilation of creative ideas in schools and colleges informally would be beneficial until a scheme at National Level is framed?

Answer: Yes, surely. My suggestion is that in each school and college, a "Bank of Creative Ideas", should be started and set up. A student, a teacher or an employee may enter his constructive ideas in a register or may note down his creative idea on a piece of paper and put the same in a special box kept for this purpose. In my view, the schools/society shall be benefitted at large.

Question: Please tell us why the Government of India have not so far given serious thought for starting a bank of ideas despite of your persistent efforts and appeals for the last 15 years?

Answer: It may be due to lack of seriousness of previous government but fortunately Modi Government promptly appreciated the importance and significance of such an institution for economic growth and social change. Thus, the "Bank of Ideas and Innovations (BII)" was established. Fortunately, it was formally inaugurated by Former President of India Dr. A.P.J. Abdul Kalam on 14 August, 2014.

Questions

1. Is role of creative ideas beneficial in Nation Building?
2. Can you please state names of some great scientists who supported the proposal of establishment of a Bank of Creative Ideas.
3. What type of persons would be especially benefitted by the Bank of Creative Ideas?
4. Whether innovative ideas provided by students, teachers and employees may prove to be useful in developing innovative culture in the society?
5. Whether today's crazy idea may become tomorrow's reality?

> *"Creativity is thinking up new things. Innovation is doing new things."*
>
> **—Theodore Levitt**

> *"The dream is not what you see in sleep. The dream is the thing which does not let you sleep."*
>
> **—Dr. A.P.J. Abdul Kalam**

Points to Ponder

1. Please write, first of all, the gist of this chapter and thereafter answer each and every question clearly.
2. In case of any clarification, please do consult your mentor or write to the author of this book at the address given at the end of this book.
3. Suggestion, if any, to improve this chapter may please be sent to the author.

□

18

A Call for Students and Youth

> Innovation is a process associated with every activity of life. A new idea may arise at any moment in the mind of a person that may prove to be useful in making the society prosperous. It also makes life simple and easy.

However, keeping in view the modern needs of India, the innovations are not only required urgently but also innovative talents must be nurtured from the very beginning and supported at every level. Moreover, the innovation as a subject must be included in the course so that an innovator at the school level may be encouraged and empowered. It has been accepted in the world that innovation is in fact a skill that can be developed like an Art.

Successful commercialization of an innovation does bring not only prosperity, honours and glory but it also becomes a source of wealth thereby paving the path of economic growth and development. Therefore, it must be our endeavour that our students and youth are ignited with innovative fire so that they may become successful innovators in future.

In this matter, we must have a clear goal that creativity must become our nature, constructiveness must become our habit, and seeds of inquisitiveness must sprout every day and every moment. Based on the above characteristics, innovation becomes our practice and enrichment of innovative activities becomes the goal and mission of all of us. We all must pray so jointly.

If our youth have yearning to do something new or to develop a new product, article, equipment or process and want to become a successful innovator they would have to choose a new path which is not even and full of hardships but it would lead them to their desired goal. This new path built by way of restlessness, ambitions and a kind of madness would certainly lead them towards their happy goal. Therefore, they shall, within their inner self, have:

"To Sow the seeds of restlessness,
To feed with manure of ambitions,
To irrigate them with water of madness."

The work is not simple and pleasant one but an innovator has to struggle to achieve his goal and fulfil his dream. It is not possible to opt for a short cut in order to achieve the success. Several dangers may have to be faced on the way.

Questions

1. Is there a lack of talents in our country? How to discover and support them so that they may become successful innovators in future?

2. Will it be beneficial for students to incorporate the subject of innovation in the school syllabus?
3. Is the innovation a skill that can be developed like an Art?
4. What type of clear objectives a successful innovator should have?
5. Is the path of a successful innovator simple and easy? If not, what types of hardships he would have to face?
6. What type of struggle an innovator has to face to achieve his desired goal?

"Learning leads to acquisition of knowledge which blossom into original thinking. Thinking leads to creativity. Creativity results in innovations. The seed of innovations are laid when one begins to question–why, how and why not. Therefore, children must be encouraged to question so as to encourage their creativity and innovative spirits."

—Dr. A.P.J. Abdul Kalam

"There's a way to do it better... find it."

—Thomas A. Edison

"Stay Hungry .... Stay Foolish".

—Steve Jobs

Points to Ponder

1. Please write, first of all, the gist of this chapter

and thereafter answer each and every question clearly.

2. In case of any clarification, please do consult your mentor or write to the author of this book at the address given at the end of this book.
3. Suggestion, if any, to improve this chapter may please be sent to the author.

Author's Address:
Vigyan Ratna Lakshman Prasad
3/6, Marris Road,
Mendu Compound,
Aligarh-202001 (U.P.) India
Tel.: 0571-2502156, Mob.: 09358626917
E-mail: lakshmanratna@yahoo.co.in

□□□